DISCOVER
The Midwest Region

by Barbara Brannon

Table of Contents

Introduction

The **Midwest region** has twelve states. The Midwest region has the Great **Lakes**. The Midwest has the Mississippi **River**.

NA

CANADA

NORTH DAKOTA

MINNESOTA

Black Hills

Great Plains

SOUTH DAKOTA

Minneapolis •

WISCONSIN

IOWA

NEBRASKA

Central Plains

RADO

Great Plains

ILLINOI

Central Plains

KANSAS

MISSOURI

Words to Know

crops

lakes

Midwest

plains

region

river

Lake Superior

CANADA

MICHIGAN

Lake Huron

Lake Michigan

MICHIGAN

• Milwaukee

Detroit •

Lake Erie

• Cleveland

• Chicago

OHIO

INDIANA

• Indianapolis

WEST VIRGINIA

▲ This is the Midwest region.

See the Glossary on page 22.

What Does the Land Look Like?

The Midwest region has **plains**.

▲ Plains are in the Midwest region.

The Midwest region has hills.

▲ Hills are in the Midwest region.

The Midwest region has lakes.

▲ Lake Michigan is in the Midwest region.

The Midwest region has rivers.

▲ The Ohio River is in the Midwest region.

The Midwest region has forests.

▲ The Manistee Forest is in the Midwest region.

What Does the Midwest Region Produce?

The Midwest region produces **crops**. The Midwest region produces wheat.

▲ The Midwest has wheat.

The Midwest region produces corn.

▲ The Midwest has corn.

The Midwest region produces milk. The Midwest region produces cheese.

Did You Know?

The Midwest is famous for cheese. People use milk to make cheese.

▲ The Midwest has cows.

The Midwest region produces cars.

car

▲ The Midwest has cars.

The Midwest region produces trucks.

truck

It's a Fact

Henry Ford built cars in Detroit, Michigan. He built his first car in 1899.

▲ The Midwest has trucks.

What Places Does the Midwest Have?

The Midwest has big cities.

▲ Chicago is in the Midwest.

The Midwest has small towns.

▲ Ely is in the Midwest.

It's a **Fact**

Ely is in Minnesota.
Many lakes are
near Ely.

13

The Midwest has farms.

▲ This farm is in the Midwest.

The Midwest has factories.

▲ This factory is in the Midwest.

14

The Midwest has dairy farms.

▲ This dairy farm is in the Midwest.

15

The Midwest has universities.

▲ This university is in the Midwest.

The Midwest has music studios.

▲ This music studio is in the Midwest.

Conclusion

The Midwest region has interesting places.

These places are in the Midwest.

18

Concept Map

Midwest Region

What Does the Land Look Like?

plains

hills

lakes

rivers

forests

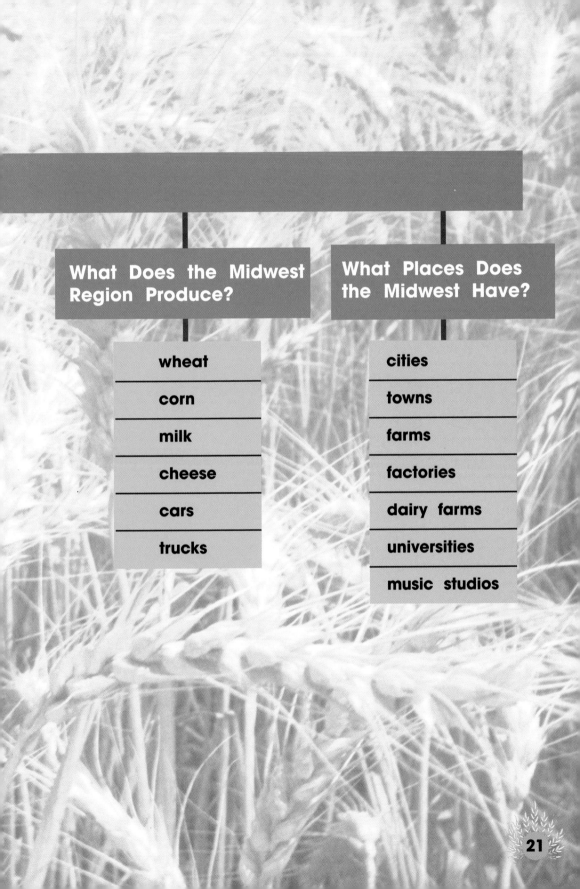

What Does the Midwest Region Produce?

wheat

corn

milk

cheese

cars

trucks

What Places Does the Midwest Have?

cities

towns

farms

factories

dairy farms

universities

music studios

Glossary

crops plants grown for food

*The Midwest region has **crops**.*

lakes bodies of water with land around them

*The Midwest region has **lakes**.*

Midwest part of the United States

*The **Midwest** region produces cars.*

plains flat land with few trees

*The Midwest region has **plains**.*

region an area of land

*The Midwest **region** has forests.*

river a long, moving body of water

*The Midwest has the Ohio **River**.*

Index